HOW TO BUILD A
BUSINESS EMPIRE
WITHOUT EXTERNAL FUNDING

CHIDI OGUEGBU
EFE OGUEGBU

HOW TO BUILD A BUSINESS EMPIRE WITHOUT EXTERNAL FUNDING

WRITTEN BY
CHIDI OGUEGBU and EFE OGUEGBU
chidi.pcfng@gmail.com

Published by:
COMMUNE WRITERS INT'L
www.communewriters.com
+234 8139 260 389

Published in the Federal Republic of Nigeria

TABLE OF CONTENT

INTRODUCTION

"I don't have the capital."

"Nobody wants to give me capital."

"The banks have turned me down five times."

These are some of the most common reasons people give for not starting or growing their businesses.
Business owners ask lots of questions about money ranging from: How do I get money to start my business? Where can I get a loan to finance my business? And so many others.
Most times, these questions are borne out of frustration and not knowing what next to do. However, the main question should be - **How can I build my business regardless of the obvious financial limitations?**

Over time, we have encountered people who complained bitterly about how they are unable to achieve their dreams and desires due to a lack of external funds or being eligible to take loans for their ideas and businesses.
It is really sad seeing those dreams shattered due to lack of a strategy that could help and pave the way for them. But not to worry, if you are in this category after you digest these tips, your story will change.

Efe and I have been running several businesses together for a long time and quite frankly, we have made lots of mistakes and gotten our fingers burnt countless times.

In 2014, we set out to start a business in Port Harcourt, Nigeria and just like a lot of other entrepreneurs and aspiring entrepreneurs, we were stuck and not able to make progress because every bank we turned to for a loan slammed their doors in our faces and it wasn't because we didn't have a sound business plan, clear steps to revenue generation or personal character.
It was because banks (and investors generally) are hardly ever impressed and enthusiastic about an unproven business; they want to give their money to a profitable, fast growing and successful business. When your business eventually hits this hallmark, they will literally seek you out, come knocking on your door and offering you loans.

Ironically, the best way to qualify for a loan is to not need one.

This pattern in the business landscape today should tell you something - you need to take your business/idea off the ground by yourself, using other creative means without focusing solely on capital or the lack of it thereof before anyone can take you seriously.

This is known as BOOTSTRAPPING - building a business with personal funds, which most times, is too little to amount to "anything".

Self-funding your business is not an easy feat, certainly not for the faint-hearted. The self-funded journeys aren't glamorous. They're not dramatic. Most publications aren't going to risk their brand to talk about it. The self-funded entrepreneurs often build their businesses as underdogs, with more concern for how their products/services run.

Of course, not every startup can be self-sufficient and you may/may not need to raise capital in the future to scale up; business is never one-size-fits-all.

However, these self-funded business owners who have striven through & come out on top, remind us to question almost everything the startup media preaches, starting with: **"Why are we seeking external funding in the first place?"**

You might be wondering, is it possible to start and grow my business without external funding?

The answer to this, albeit surprising is a big fat YES! It is very possible and quite rewarding too.

The Bootstrappers' Mindset is a mindset that every entrepreneur must have whether you have an abundance of capital or not - a mindset to solve problems creatively, with the cheapest, frugal and agile means possible; going all out for the achievement of a vision as a result of a profound conviction about it.

We know you are eager to know how possible that could be.

Well, read on. This e-book will do justice to that and give you tips on how to start and grow your business or empire with no external funding.

CHAPTER I

THE IMPORTANCE OF MONEY

No doubt money is essential to anything you want to build. There is little or nothing money does not play an important role in.

Cash is important for your business to survive. A business that lacks funding and money will eventually kick the bucket.

Cash is also important because it later becomes the payment for things that make your business run; expenses like stock or raw materials, employees, rent, utility etc.

Needless to say, money is a necessary ingredient needed for your business to scale through. Therefore the question is not whether you need money to build your business; the question is -

1. How do I generate money for my business without seeking external factors like taking a loan or inviting investors into my business &
2. How can I make the most value out of the money that I have?

Well, the quick answer to the above questions are:

1. To have paying customers &
2. To spend wisely respectively.

These two must be at the back of your mind as a bootstrapping entrepreneur.

Our Story

When we started The Paper Packaging Company (www.tppcng.com), we started out selling only paper cups that we imported from overseas and as time went by, our customers wanted them branded with their logos/photos on them. Of course at that point, we didn't have the means or know-how to achieve it.

After contacting our suppliers overseas, we were left with 2 options - either to invest in machines (in excess of $100,000) or purchase branded cups directly from suppliers and wait longer months (4 months) to receive them.

Neither of these options were feasible to us as we didn't have the money to invest in the machines (as you know, the banks were a no-go area) & our customers could not wait that long to have their products but we knew we had to sell to survive.

We creatively began to study the paper cup. Just like a curious child would do, we took the 1st cup, tore it open to understand its workings. Then we took the 2nd and the 3rd and even up to the 20th cup! After a couple of days, we were ready to try out branding the cup ourselves by hand. YES! You read that right….by hand!

It took a lot of practice but after a couple of failed attempts, we became PROs at branding paper cups by hand and subsequently increased our branding capacity. If you were not told, you would think a machine did the job.

With this, we were able to meet our growing customer demands, **generate revenue without breaking the bank** and with just a few inexpensive readily available materials.

This right here is the Bootstrappers' Mindset!

This is the mindset that self-funded entrepreneurs have - the mindset to solve problems creatively.

Money is not the solution to all the challenges you will experience in your business. You must be ready to think deeply and creatively, roll up your sleeves, get your hands dirty and do the work.

Your business challenge might not be the same as ours but the principle is the same and it works universally.

"An entrepreneur does more than anyone thinks possible with less than anyone thinks possible" - John Doer

Having money to run your business is important and you can achieve that without seeking external funding.

You can combine the tips below to build your business from the ground up.

We do hope by the time you finish this e-book; your perspective will shift and focus on the little things that add up to make you build a successful business.

Let's get into it!

CHAPTER 2

THE BOOTSTRAPPER'S GUIDE: 3 TIPS FOR BOOTSTRAPPING YOUR BUSINESS TO SUCCESS

When we first started our company, The Paper Packaging Company (TPPC) about 5 years ago, we didn't know that any such word as "bootstrapping" existed.

All we knew was that we had an idea which later transformed into a vision that we were 101% convinced about, so we were willing to risk EVERYTHING for the actualisation of that vision, regardless of the many shut doors and limited resources.

Our experiences, mistakes and lessons would be useless if we do not pass it down in forms of teachings, mentoring, coaching, books, courses etc. to people who are walking the path that we took and the many others who would walk that same path in the future.

The principles we are about to share with you have worked consistently at TPPC and we have been able to generate revenue in excess of N200 Million over a period of 4years without external funding using these same principles.

So you see, this is doable...if we did it, so can you too!

3 TIPS FOR BOOTSTRAPPING YOUR BUSINESS TO SUCCESS

Communication:

We consider this one of the most important boxes to tick on the Bootstrapper's Guide.

Businesses are born out of a vision to offer value to its customers. The value could be a product, a service or a combination of both. However, that value is useless if it does not get to the set of persons it was created for. The only way it can get to them is via communication.

Your communication must be on 2 levels and both communications must be done effectively and on a budget to ensure that your business doors are open with the lights on.

i.   **Internal Communication**

You might be a one-man team now but that would not be for too long except you want to burn out and eventually go out of business.

Your business and its value offering is as good as your team. Making a great team involves communicating your business vision very explicitly and in simple ways that each member of your team understands and knows exactly what to do to deliver on the business value offerings to customers.

It is also important to note that the higher your vision, the more connected people are to it. The vision of your business must serve a higher purpose, a purpose greater than you as an entrepreneur that continually inspires not just you, but every member of your team.

Can you link your business' vision to one of the Sustainable Development Goals (SDGs)?

Does your business vision positively impact other people?

These are great ways to keep yourself and members of your team inspired and committed to the vision.

ii.   External Communication

Now that you have created this exceptional value, your customers need to hear about it, they need to know that the solution to their burning problems and pains is with you and they need to get it from you.

These times are the best times for you to be in business because you can communicate with your customers on the Internet for free. Platforms like YouTube, Instagram,

WhatsApp, Facebook etc. are all absolutely free and are great resources to leverage on to spread the word about your business.

Even without a marketing budget, you can get customers irresistibly drawn to your brand through storytelling so much so that they become your micro-influencers and market for you.
People buy into other people and their stories!!!

Once you have the 1st, 2nd, 10th and many more customers, get their feedback on your product/service, improve on it based on the feedback gotten and you are sure to have referrals from them.

As a self-funded business, 2 things must ring constantly in your head:
- How do I keep attracting paying customers? &
- Does my team know what to do?

During the first 4 years of our operations in TPPC, we did not have a marketing budget. All of our customers came from the different social media platforms we engaged with and referrals from existing customers.

We focused more on building a customer-centric brand, one that really cared about customers and took their feedback as a privilege and an opportunity to learn, improve and grow.

We also did a lot of work communicating the vision of our brand to everyone (even those that didn't care to listen) through stories and linking our vision to a purpose greater than us.

For instance, we are an organisation that manufactures food packaging. We could have presented our value offering that way to our customers but a higher vision was linking our brand story to sustainability and how every purchase of our product each customer makes is a step towards achieving a cleaner and healthier environment for us all.

Effective communication is one of the most powerful tools a bootstrapper can use to gain raving mad fans out of customers and employees.

Collaboration
Collaboration means to work with another person or a group of persons to achieve a goal/purpose.

Anyone can come up with an idea for a business but it will take the collaboration of many people to make it successful; from employees to mentors to partners to vendors and other stakeholders.

No great business has ever been built solo, yours would not be the first. Even if you tried to go solo, your business might never live to tell the story.

The business world is complex & success in it requires multiple and dynamic skills, capabilities and experiences; many of which you may not have as an entrepreneur or as a business.

At the core of every business, is the coordination of various activities from different members of the organisation to ultimately deliver value in form of a product/service to customers. Business is all about collaboration.

This might sound very simple and easy to do. However, what really makes it work is the mindset behind it and that is what we have found to be the most challenging part for most entrepreneurs especially those in Africa because of issues of trust.

To collaborate effectively, you must possess a mindset that is willing to share victories and wins with others and not mind taking 20% of something great as opposed to taking 100% of nothing at all. A mindset that does not entertain fears in having someone else in the spotlight, letting them shine in areas where they possess strength while you work behind the scenes to achieve a common goal and a mindset that is willing to get naked and build trust.

A lot of the products that we offer at TPPC require heavy machine setup to aid production costing millions of US dollars that we could not afford.

After our survey, we realised that there were a couple of big companies here in Nigeria who had those machines and we approached them, brokered a production deal that was mutually beneficial for both parties with them. Yes, our margins were not as high as it would have been had we acquired the machines ourselves but we were willing to get off the ground not having to invest heavily in machines (that we couldn't afford anyway) for a profit cut.

Doing this enabled us to increase production capacity at a very accelerated rate in the shortest time possible and increase our sales tremendously.

There are so many ways you could collaborate with others in line with your business needs. The key thing is to note that every collaboration should be mutually beneficial and towards a common goal.

Creativity

This is the most important skill needed to succeed as an entrepreneur and more importantly, a bootstrapping entrepreneur.

Creativity is the life line of your business and it enables you to come up with new ideas and strategies that give you competitive advantage to aid your business success. Your product or service offering might not be novel but how you creatively differentiate yourself from other businesses offering the same products/service is what makes you stand out in a crowded market attracting paying customers.

An unwavering commitment to your business vision despite obvious limitations fuels your creativity to get things done innovatively without settling for defeat.

In one of the stories above, we shared how with no money and a burning desire to grow the business, we started branding paper cups by hand. Honestly, maybe if we had the money at the time, we would have invested it in a cup making machine at first thought not knowing that there was a cheaper and creative alternative that would yield the same result and help us scale at our level.

Our supposed financial limitation pushed us into critical thinking and subsequently, innovation (the action) to make our goal achieved regardless and till now, we question every investment ensuring that there is no cheaper and more creative alternative.

Do not stop at creative thinking, take innovative actions in line with your creative thoughts and make magic.

That is the Bootstrappers' Mindset!!!

Most times, your limitations are blessings in disguise forcing you to think more creatively...embrace it.

Harvard Business Review sums it up this way;
"Learning to improvise is essential to startup success and it's hard to learn unless it's forced upon you. Bootstrapping does just that."

CHAPTER 3

CASE STUDY EXAMPLES

Shutter Stock

Jon Oringer was a professional software developer and an amateur photographer. He combined this set of skills and used 30,000 photos from his personal photo library to start a stock photo service that is currently worth $2 billion dollars. His capital efficiency paid off and ultimately turned him into a truly self-made billionaire.

Calendly

Also, Tope Awotona founded Calendly, an online scheduling app in 2013, with no external funding. He raided his bank account to launch Calendly in 2013. Eventually, he ran out of money and started to seek external funding and every search led to a slammed door in his face.

In his words;

"It forced me to become resourceful, scrappy, and maniacally focused. I learned how to stretch each dollar."

The business is approaching $30 million in recurring revenue, and growing more than 100 percent year-over-year. It's been profitable since 2016 and he is the majority owner.

CHAPTER 4

CONCLUSION

Bootstrapping is not a sprint.
It's a marathon requiring endurance and tenacity.

- Start small
- Don't rush
- Avoid comparing yourself with others
- Minimize the pressure
- Learn as you go
- Time is your greatest asset...USE IT!!!

ABOUT THE AUTHORS

CHIDI

Chidi Oguegbu holds a Bachelor's Degree in Petroleum Engineering from University of Ibadan, Oyo State and a Diploma in Mineral Resources Engineering from Petroleum Training Institute, Effurun, Warri.

He has worked in various oil and gas companies in the likes of Segofs Oil services, National Petroleum Investment Management Services (NAPIMS), National Petroleum Development Company (NPDC) and Total Nigeria Limited.

He completed his National Youth Service Corps (NYSC) with Zenith Bank Plc where he grabbed the fundamental principles applied in the banking and financial sector in Nigeria.

He is the Co-Founder/CEO of The Paper Packaging Company an organization focused on reducing the adverse effects of single-use plastics on the planet and providing a compostable alternative to plastic/nylon food packaging.

EFE

Eferobosa Mabel Oguegbu is an accounting and finance expert with over 8 years' experience in the finance industry. She is currently the Co-Founder and Director of Finance at The Paper Packaging Company, a Company focused on reducing the adverse effects of single use plastic on the environment by providing eco-friendly biodegradable food packaging solutions. She has been able to add unique value through application of her experience in financial accounting/reporting, budget and cost control, business process audit, assurance, internal control, management and leadership to her current role.

She is passionate about reducing poverty in Nigeria and she volunteers with organisations focused on reducing poverty in Nigeria.

Lightning Source UK Ltd.
Milton Keynes UK
UKHW020748270123
416054UK00013B/1434

9 798356 828355